ANONYMOUSE

By

-Arthur White-

The mass of men serve the State thus, not as men mainly, but as machines, with their bodies. They are the standing army, and the militia, jailers, constables, posse comitatus, etc. In most cases there is no free exercise whatever of the judgment or of the moral sense.

—Henry David Thoreau, "Civil Disobedience"

MIND HIVE SOCIETY

A MODERN SLAVERY HIDDEN FROM PLAIN SIGHT.

Society has been tricked and played with for centuries, but in the recent era a new model emerged of misdirection and indoctrination was established. A new model that would keep society on check and avoid the insurrections that destroyed predecessor systems of control of the masses. As Henry David Thoreau, pointed out in his 1849 essay "Civil Disobedience" Population of a state is almost regarded as property of the state and meant to do with them whatever the industrial state needs them to do. Of course keeping society as under a simulation of free will in an enslaved model. A slave model in which humanity has accepted and agreed upon happily. A system that controls what society can do and can believe in. But it does it in a far more elegant and hidden manner.

Any child told what to do and what not to do will eventually do what has been forbidden to him. Rebellion and breaking free is the natural instinct. Defiance of the rules has a certain romantic idea in it. So how do you control and avoid society from rebelling or questioning?

A new and better model of control had to be established. One that made people see restrictions and measures of control as something they would be eager and happy to participate in. The physical chains and the whips will eventually make slaves rebel. But if society willingly chained themselves and forced themselves into submission then no threat of rebellion would ever occur.

People look back to the dark ages and wonder how humanity believed all that it had been told. From inquisition trials to oppressive rulers and information blackouts. But we now look into our own period of time and we can affirm we live in an equally dark era to middle ages although practically hidden from plain sight, A darkness simulated as freedom of choice, equality and freedom of speech which as we will go through further on explain how such things are simple simulations to keep a modern working slave force under the idea that it lives in freedom.

Society is slowly stripped away from individual thinking and pushed towards collective social programming. Individuality is hard to control, Collective thinking must prevail to keep society under control. The mind hive Forcing behaviors and common ideas in the group. This Behavior seen in bees and ants keeping them at the service of the colony (Nation, group). A forced collectivity that removes different forms of thinking and replaces them with a one state of mind giving birth to an invisible control over what the collective thinks, Social media now allows a better simulation of the mind hive. Example is when new social media challenges are made and encourages others to strip themselves of their identity to form part of a collective. Seems fun so let's follow, People soon hop in to the new funny curios trend. A face that ages you becomes trendy, nothing sinister about having fun they will say except soon you have millions replicating one another's behavior. Train your colony to react and replicate one another's behavior as a fun gimmick and when you least know it everyone behaves, thinks and likes what the rest of the colony does.

Soon everyone hops into whatever trend is placed on them convincing them its free will. Freedom is stripped away and now you can convince the colony to agree with whatever way of life is carried out by the rest and in their best interest. The colony now believes in the programed idea and will protect that idea at all cost. Locking itself in a prison without bars, no locks, no walls. Chained to the idea that what the collective does is the only way to live. Anyone living or thinking outside the collective mind hive system is an outcast and must be punished for doing so.

The magic trick is not just taking away free will and individuality from society. The real magic trick is doing it in a way that people willingly surrender free will and they do it gladly and with a big smile.

The Banksy's Zodiac show
or
Mutilate you way into fame.

Let us take now a second and examine the phenomenon behind Banksy. Fame is an asset craved by many gained by few. It turns instantly the mediocre into influencer in this carnival modern world. To excel in this carnival, Talent is not a requirement, only the shock it creates in the numb crowd. Shock by mutilation is a well-known tactic employed by the modern entertainers. If you can't succeed in life due to lack of talent then mutilate your way into fame. Shock audiences by mutilating what is convention and expected. Mutilate the established order. Famed street artist has been known to shock audiences by desecrating cultural well known images all under the premise of so called bringing awareness. Society needs to be shocked, It removes the monotonous routine of life. Works better if you make people think they become cool if they attach themselves to certain ideas.

Like any theatrical spectacle the shaman, clown, magician must remain anonymous under the cloak of a disguise, a mask. If his identity were to be revealed the magic and wonder falls from the imaginary fantasy to the boredom of mortality. Myth and legend is born. Entertainment, sells in every form, Gossip, fear, disaster and of course the marvel of show business. The bigger the lights the more the bugs are attracted to it. The glimmer of the spectacle. Shiny bright lights outside the premier promising your numb life will receive a feast of wonder.

Trick is to shock and to shock with what's not expected. The pole caps melting is not a shock. Its expected to happen because ice melts. What's a shock is a Zodiac killer, An Anonymous dark being who appears out of nowhere, unexpected leaving a very morbid entertainment of messages on his path. A mutilation of the ordinary daily life and routines. Just like Banksy, another anonymous mysterious figure whose fame comes from defacing and mutilating well known images leaving a trail on walls with messages for the entertainment of his followers. And so the trail of mutilation gains strength with even more entertaining stunts such as shredding art at an auction. And so Banksy in a well planned and coordinated stunt captures the numb audience's attention with a new gimmick turning a mediocre painting into a show and therefore increasing its monetary value and fame status. Mutilation of the ordinary has become the new entertainment. It sells tickets and t-shirts for the bored numb society. While talented artists who spent years studying artistic techniques never gain attraction due to the lack of show around them, entertainers like Banksy gain stardom with less talent just by mutilating their way into fame. Of course Banksy must remain anonymous just like the Zodiac or Jack the Ripper because it creates a spectacle.

Mutilation gains power, Masses are entertained and just like any No talented serial killer whose only merit was to create a show around his trail of death and therefore the mutilation giving fame. The bigger the show around the mutilation act the more it will spread. It's no fun to simply sell a painting at an auction. It doesn't attract the bored masses into gossip. But to mutilate it and shred it as its being sold now that's what makes the crowds rejoice and gossip. When the Banksy serial mutilator loses relevance just like any serial killer a new wave of mutilation and controversy spectacle is needed in the service of gaining fame and keeping itself on the public eye. Knowingly they lack any real talent to succeed in the world except that of being self-publicist at all cost. If you lack talent just mutilate yourself into fame.

Tragedy and mutilation sells newspapers and fills TV screens, it's the main dish on social media. You don't have people glued to their TV Screens or mobile phones because penguins walk the frozen Antarctica,

You need to exterminate violently an entire penguin community, shot in 4K so you can see the gritty details of the massacre. The more violent and cruel the event the more the televised feast. The more shares it gets on social media. The violence of the coliseum. The actor going to prison. The Celebrity divorce scandal.

You could have the greatest artwork published on Instagram or at an art exhibition that almost no one will be paying attention to it, No news channel will cover the unveiling of the artwork but shred a mediocre stencil artwork at an auction and the world goes crazy. The mediocre circus performers as Banksy gaining fame while real talented disappears into oblivion. In the end it's not Banksy's fault, he simply knows how to trick and entertain a numb worldwide audience.

ANONYMOUSE

THE REBELLION, JUSTICE AND FREEDOM SHOW.

"What the eyes see and the ears hear, the mind believes."

— D. H. Lawrence

"Has the world gone mad or have we've just fooled ourselves too long with a fake sanity?"

Maybe those who have been called insane are the little few who have seen the absurdity and lunacy of a world bound by a mad society. A world of happy slaves that will fight to the death to defend their own prison. A world indoctrinated since birth, a world of fashionable morals.

Since the establishment of society, rules have been created to keep order. Some rules more tyrannical than others, some meant to oppress its population, other rules based on its local religious beliefs. Some rules have pushed society to commit atrocities and mass murder of those who did not comply. In recent times society has seen catastrophic events unfold, Today we see division has increased to levels of hatred similar to those of pre WW2 era. Social media has made the world be far more connected and news travels at speeds unseen before. A world in which information is accessed with very little effort.

Information that can benefit or can be used to push society where it is desired.

Society was created as a means of survival. The word FEAR is imprinted in its roots. Fear of what lays outside the walls of the built structure. An invisible wall that keeps all demons at bay. Order and Chaos. For the invisible wall to sustain itself, demons must be harvested, fashioned and refashioned. Threats that endanger the established order need to occur with a constant flow. Without those threats governing rules collapse, the structure that holds society under a leash may crumble. Opposing forces must be nurtured for the invisible wall that keeps the flock under control to subsist. Fear and threat of what lays outside the indoctrinated world is constantly fed to is inhabitants like any gardener planting seeds and watering them consistently so the idea of chaos outside the wall thrives. Great care to not drown them or leave them dry. And so the of communism was planted, A ghost that communism was coming for you. They fed its dread to the established social order."

"When communism failed as a threat new terrors had to be developed. Outside the wall only cold and suffering exists. Very similar to telling a child stories of all those little young boys abducted by witches and strangers. A child needs to be fed fear for him to not wonder alone into the forest. And so society in dread of the chaos outside the wall will fight to the death to keep the invisible wall standing.

As civilization grew, cities guarded by fortresses were constructed, Walls kept foreign intruders away. Inside its walls the fabric of society was crafted and molded to fit its contemporary religious beliefs and moral values. And so an invisible WALL of ideas and norms was erected in these cities. An invisible barrier created for society to remain in its place. Its bricks and mortar are the moral and religious set of rules given by the establishment. A set of limits and rules that had to be accepted You are told not to cross that WALL, if do so excommunication to a world outside the social established Wall where all the terrors of the world will hunt you down for failing to comply with the order and beliefs you are forced to obey unquestionably. To keep people behind that wall examples of punishment and ridicule are systematically carried out by those who have created the invisible Wall. The construct of that wall changes as morality moves through fashion but always preserving its initial purpose of keeping its flock under a leash.

In the old days interracial marriages were considered a moral felony. A moral set of rules that were part of that WALL. He who broke the sanctity of the holy social consensus were severely punished. Keeping races separated and making sure no one stepped out of line. Laws placed and unquestioned as being wrong and cruel. Even if laws had not been put in place, society would enforce separation by any means. Society made sure the WALL and its morality remained untouched. Society itself became judge and jury. To commit the crime of interracial mixing meant being cast outside the wall. So you either remained in line or you would face excommunication from inside the wall. Similar situation occurred with gays in society. Forced to remain in the dark by fear of losing its livelihood and face attacks and imprisonment. Society in its protection of moral fashion values never questioned the draconian ruthless laws enforced on society with different sexual preference. The WALL had to be guarded at all cost. Prison persecution and public shaming if necessary to keep the Wall standing.

Society is told what needs to be told, limiting their inquiry of a different perspective outside the established wall. By isolating people to certain beliefs society becomes unaware to different perspectives and ideas. Without perspective truth can't be discovered nor seen. The flock becomes ignorant of different ideas. The flock is left with only one side of the story.

In law perspective is necessary to find the truth. Each side gives its account on the situation at hand to a Jury. Jury hears both sides and then makes its mind. Society, religion and government bans perspective from its citizens keeping them in darkness for its own benefit.

If you don't have contradictory opinions truth is whatever you say truth to be.

You can't question Capitalism or Communism or the ideas and teachings of a religion or sexual preference if different ideas are banned. Like any authoritarian system you limit the information anyone can have and force into public shaming or judgment for questioning different ideas.

 Society once it accepts that which is being told and enforced to them under the premise that its for their own good, then the social group will become guardian on its own. Fear of shame. Fear of being outcast by their own social group. Fear of crossing the established WALL will keep society in its place. Fear of rejection, slowly society becomes its own police under the dread of upsetting the established order.

The fear of being cast out outside the WALL. A WALL people believe so much in, a WALL that was created for them. A WALL in which fashion, morality, religion and the contemporary values are kept and guarded. Each member of the social group becomes judge and jury of their own cell and they will do it with a smile.

NEW SLAVERY

HIDDEN FROM PLAIN SIGHT

"What the eye doesn't see and the mind doesn't know, doesn't exist."

—Harry Houdini

Society is constructed under the basis of obedience, Obedience to the established order. Similar to ant and bee colonies all working in service of the established order. Following orders from the Queen in the beehive. Eventually if the bees become too suffocated by a tyrannical system, figures of liberation rise. The bees need their basic needs and demands covered to avoid rebellion and return to conformism. When basic needs are not met then chaos and anarchy rises. In theory the bee society will want more than what they have, a principal of human greed inherit in survival mechanisms across time. But in reality society is too lazy and scared to undertake the rigorous ordeals that greed requires them to get that which they desire.

For social establishment to succeed inside the wall the hive needs to provide enough to its inhabitants. It keeps the bees in a struggle and codependent of its queen. If the bees had no need then the colony would eventually collapse. So who is the Queen in the beehive? Is it a group? It would be too easy to single it out as a group. Conspiracy theorist need to put a face to the prison guard. The Queen is a far simpler concept. Its an Idea, the idea becomes ideal, ideal turns into canon, canon becomes reality. The idea of religion, the idea of nation, the idea of a flag. Idea of perfect family, perfect road to success. Ideas as abstract and empty as thinking the world was flat. But that idea became what dictated the way of life of entire generations, anyone opposing such idea went against the establishment of the colony.

Idea that slavery was right and acceptable marked the way certain humans were treated for centuries. That Idea that only certain humans deserved rights. The idea that Jews should be exterminated. Ideas that can become dangerous and sinister or kind and benevolent.

Ideas are molded, guarded and fought for. People in inside their prison walls are constantly fed ideas. Ideas that keep them inside their cage and anything that upsets their indoctrinated ideals upsets the established order. Ideas and their nature are fashionable and change from time to time. Just like Romans incorporated new ideologies and beliefs into their society avoiding direct confrontation and instead mutating into new ways of thought making it possible for their acquired territories to join easier into the empire.

The idea of the value of things, the value of people, the idea of the value of money and gold. Entire generations have enslaved themselves in pursuit of ideas and many have died defending them. Nazi Germany gave its people an idea and fed it to them to the point they committed the most hideous atrocities in the service of those ideas. So in this quest of validating an idea and protecting it you must create a system that guards dissident ideas from emerging. Once an idea has been inoculated into a social group, it will defend it even if the idea is insane. Anyone from the outside who has not been infected by the idea has different perspective. Few reject the inoculation of ideas. Few question what is being told to them. Dissident ideology rising must be taken into equation.

And the question rises. How do you control those few who may come forward to free people from an idea if society is its own Judge, Jury and Prison guard at the same time? You control those few who may question the wall and its establishment?"

The solution is far simpler. Simulation of freedom fighters as Robin Hood, Zorro, Anonymous, a masked figure which defends the poor oppressed. Under the premise of course that the masked figure hides his identity against the oppressors.

ROBIN HOOD AND ANNONYMOUS

The use of theatricality and Spectacle. Truth becomes a spectacle. If you don't turn it into a spectacle the numb crowds will hardly ever pay attention. Crowds don't want the truth they want gladiators to kill themselves for their entertainment" For the coliseum to work a show must take place and that's where Zorro comes in play. A masked figure popping up in televised broadcast spectacle interrupting the continuity of the everyday routine with a threat. Suddenly the ordinary becomes a show. Of course the selected targets never really put the establishment on a real crisis.

 "When needed, Zorro will burn at the stake a few scapegoats to give validity to the cause.

Like any Ponzi scheme or scam you need to give up certain truths to make the scammed person think he is actually getting genuine information all the time. Give a few earnings to solidify the belief that the scheme is actually real. Theatricality of a magician, Show the audience what you want while you misdirect their attention towards the real trick. Create a big show on every presentation. The theatrical mask or the cape of the Zorro. A trail of Messages from the masked figure. Soon like any serial killer leaving a trail of blood on its path making people take for granted everything the killer says is true. No reason to doubt anymore what is being said to them. After all the Zorro never gave his identity to make him accountable about anything he said the simulation of truth and justice suddenly became real and unquestionable in the collective mind. People invest emotionally and believe so much on the Zorro figure that they can't question anymore what it says or does. The crowd has given up their power of questioning and become obedient once again to what is being told to them.

Zorro gives its audience a dose of dopamine and excitement and a sense of liberation. They actually start to believe they are attaching themselves to the true truth. An illusion of the destruction of the wall and its oppression. A momentary liberation and sense of control and justice.

A fall guy for the masses inside the wall. A patsy for all their tears, all their frustrations. Someone they can blame for what they themselves allowed, for being too coward and lazy to question the wall. A scapegoat to all which they themselves have helped happen. Call it releasing pressure so the pressure pot doesn't explode. Society needs to put the blame on someone for their own incarceration. The more an individual holds on to the emotional investment of his prison the more he will blame others for his dire situation. Monsters need a face to crucify. Once the crowd has been satisfied it can go back to its daily routine. A new fashionable idea has been induced and inoculated into them. Unfortunately those trapped inside the prison walls don't realize they were just moved to a different prison. New painted walls give a sense of better living conditions. New flag is waved inside their prison. New incorporated ideas into their prison.

The Wall can't be broken nor torn down of course because if such a thing happened, eternal chaos would emerge and all beasts of labor inside the wall would devour themselves like a cancer. So the fall guy is created to release pressure on the inhabitants and upgrade the prison to Prison 2.1. Prison just changed the package and a few gimmicks but in essence it's the same. Windows 7 and windows 10 simply has few bugs corrected or new screen colors and gadgets in it but windows is actually the same.

After the lynching mob has been satisfied things can get back to normal and society can go back inside their own cage which they themselves close the door and lock themselves up again.

THE ROMANTIC IDEA OF THE FREEDOM FIGHTERS AND CHE GUEVARA'S OF THE WORLD

Few ever question what makes a freedom fighter figure tick, what are his real motives. How information became disclosed by them and who actually benefits from its disclosure. Why the freedom fighter attacked or hacked something. They just assume Robin Hood, Snowden, Che Guevara hero

disclosed information or carried out an attack because
he believes in liberty and Justice. Positivism instead
of realism. People in their desperation and desire for a
scapegoat will believe somehow information was
filtered by some heroic freedom fighter greater than
themselves. But was information actually filtered?
Was the freedom fighter actually working to tear
down the wall of oppression? Or was our heroic
freedom fighter just a pawn to refashion the prison
WALL in which the social construct has locked itself?
The idea that a freedom fighter emerged without a
personal hidden reason can be as absurd as believing
politicians kiss babies because they all have
tenderness and unselfish interest. What the eyes see
and the ears hear the mind believes. Magic trick has
been sold and its better sold if you turn the hero into a
victim. The crucifixion allows the victim to gain
popularity and to make the simulated freedom fight
real.

The US couldn't join a World War 2 because the
popular consensus went against it, so the easiest way
to convince the population is to push the enemy
around until he hits you in the nose and then you can
say. You see he's the violent one. He punched me and
of course approval for attack against Japan and
Germany occurs unquestionably. If Pearl Harbor
attack had been frustrated and prevented then maybe
the nationwide idea of going to war would have not
met such approval and enthusiasm. If Snowden had
not been persecuted then maybe what he had said

would have been irrelevant. Truth is most people don't even know what Snowden is they just now he

Of course the stories of selfless sacrificial heroes who fought tyranny is a nice romantic idea. It sells t-shirts and makes good movies. Remember the Alamo propaganda. Not everything is Black and white and not everything is what it seems. The propaganda machine gives heroes a quasi-messianic status. Free of flaws and greed. Virtue is instantly splattered among the idol.

Find victims so the crowd can empathize with them. Build monuments around their attached virtue. The social propaganda circus has its victim face and its monster mask.

Instantly the crowd attaches itself to the victim and distances itself from the monster. Anyone who could doubt the validity of the victim or his almost saint status is met with the iron fist of social justice. The thing in the end is not that the Hero figure is put in doubt or questioned for its holy virtue it is that once the individual has incorporated the hero as is model towards salvation the self can't distinguish the self apart from the hero. Going against the victim hero means going against the self. Self-preservation instincts come in play and the. Hero savior must be defended at all costs.

The Idol has been born.

SOCIAL MEDIA
OR
THE BIG BROTHER
SHOW

Big Brother, a term associated to a government or a watchful oppressive instrument in an authoritarian regime to keep an eye on its citizens. Orwell's novel spoke of a vigilant government watching and controlling its citizens. Fabricating stories to keep everyone under a tight control. Today we see the Big Brother phenomenon but not as thought to be the government watching over its people in fact is not some secret society looking over your shoulders keeping you under a leash. It is a much more real and horrifying truth. Repression doesn't come from the control room at a secret society. It comes from the own social establishment. Society is its own gatekeeper and the glue that keeps everyone trapped behind the invisible WALL created by society itself. Modern moral fashion sustain the WALL and its mortars of oppression. The all watchful eye of a brotherhood bound by a flag, a group restrained in a collective prison. For it to function you need society to be watchful of one another's moves and actions, like a clock work mechanism, all pieces moving at the rhythm they are told. It is the "look what he/she did." "Did you hear what He / she did?" "Oh and the Kardashians did this and did that." "How dare she/he say this and that?" Reactive infuriated crowds chant punishment on a daily basis from the comfort of their electronic mobile devices. Acts that seem innocent until policy and social establishment is dictated by the brotherhood of citizens surveilling and shaming one another into submission. The collective group is first dictated what the standard and current moral behavior is meant to be placed in order and society will be the very own watchdog of keeping its own members chained under its control.

Such practices can find its early forms in the dark ages under the rule of catholic authoritarian establishment. Its inquisition becoming the enforcer and guardian of the holy law and order. Its society remained vigilant and frightened of anyone who dared break the established order. Punishments were carried out publicly to warranty society saw the gruesome end the moral and religious rebels faced. In more modern times we find examples in the Soviet Union and McCarthyism in the USA. During the communist regime in Russia, the KGB kept surveillance over its population by keeping snitches in its community, carefully watching over everyone's moves and opinions. You had to be careful who you spoke to and the subjects you spoke about. You never knew who could be KGB. The West saw its fist come down on anyone accused of being a communist. And so a vigilant state emerged.

In today's social media, Society has found a new form of oppression. The vigilant eye of anyone logged into social media. The ultimate Big brother. Cameras on every phone to keep an eye on those who dare offend the established order. Do not dare to speak your mind because you will be forced to repent and lose your livelihood for offending the established order. The sharing begins, Burn the fool who dared to speak his mind. Shame him at the social media inquisition. And so social media now keeps people under a leash. There is no escaping the surveillance eye of its citizens. Shaming of any different form of thinking is now the common trait. Give a different opinion and soon memes and shaming spreads at speeds never before seen in history. Public executions occur on daily basis at the tribunals of social media. The crowd gathers to shame and bully one another into submission without trial. Throwing curses and as in ancient times throwing stones at the offender of moral and religious establishment as he is paraded through the plaza for everyone to see and point their blood thirst fingers of moral decency at those who dared offend establishment. We have traded the shaming parade in plazas and streets for the sharing of photos and videos in social media. The lynching mob cries for punishment without trial.

In this social construct, to speak your own mind is now a crime punishable by the modern thought police.

He said she said becomes the new testimony in the public execution social media trial. Ego playing a major role in these modern angry mob executions. If it's in social media then it must be true. Learning the backstory of an event is irrelevant for the visceral crowd hungry for justice at all cost.

Because of self-preservation mechanisms (One can't go against the self if you emotionally become attached to an idea therefor it must be true) the crowd then reacts instead of thinking and submitting things to analysis. Analysis requires to objectively pause and search points of perspective and doing so you eliminate visceral reaction which of course social media has very well trained people into a pattern of reaction and to help them do so it has given its social media users them emojis and happy or sad, angry and laughing REACTION faces. A perfect monkey sees monkey does society. The birth of the perfect visceral puppet and its own emojis to carry an execution.

Today's world is just as primitive as those old angry lynching mobs tearing black men to pieces for crimes they did not commit only because someone cried wolf.

Angry visceral mobs who attended executions during the French Revolution, chanting for nobility to be decapitated under the sharp blade of the guillotine. When the head rolled into basket wild chanting emerging as the mob rejoiced in pleasure. Punishment had been carried out while they say to themselves "May they be an example for their wickedness" The wicked and evil of a visceral crowd pretending to hold the ultimate truth and purity of consciousness. As the popular passage says "May he who is free of sin cast the first stone" Hypocrisy as instantly everyone in the modern social media realm begins to throw stones.

Are modern social media executions any different from those carried out in the French revolution or the inquisition? Has society even evolved from the blood thirsty animals that lynched people across time? Just same blood thirsty men and women in a frenzy of visceral vengeful emotions.

Morality which is so heavily guarded by those living inside the WALL is impermanent and changes like fashion. What is now considered immoral once may have been a common accepted moral practice and what we now consider moral may well have been immoral in the past and may become immoral in the future. The confusion of what is good and evil vs what is moral and immoral tricks the social establishment by trying to outcast a fashionable moral as if it were the outcasting of evil. At a certain period of time being gay was not only considered immoral but had to be eradicated as if its existence was the very face of evil. Gay men were tortured and burned at the stake. Public executions for everyone to see the fate of those who dared to offend moral principles. Men like Turing were chemically castrated for being gay. Free will is abolished in the name of social moral. Verdict and sentenced carried out even if it's cruel and in its essence evil. A necessity to keep the demons of homosexuality or communism or Jews or anyone who did not fit the contemporary established order behind the constructed social wall.

Questions then rise. How did society approve of public executions in the name of moral? The social establishment in order to preserve itself and the WALL, needs indoctrination, Flags to which they can identify themselves. Ego then confuses the self with the flag, the religion, the brand or whatever symbol it is made to attach itself to. Losing individuality and replacing it for a collective mind. In the collective, the individual ceases to exist. The individual's name is replaced by gender, nationality, religion, race or group. The opposing group instantly becomes alienated and detached from oneself. Them and me, Germans and Jews, Christians and Muslims, Blacks and whites, Gay and straight, Men and Women, The being can now see the being contrary to the ideals he holds as Alien outside the wall, Ego loses empathy and in consequence loses compassion for those outside its circle. Those outside the circle are instantly considered by ego as lesser beings that either comply and transform or must be destroyed. Anything that threatens the ego must be eliminated at all cost.

Of course the wall can't really sustain itself forever without revealing its bricks have been built by removing free will on the individual. The pressure sooner or later will threaten the foundations of the wall and a new construct is made, A new fashion to trick the self of an evolution of thinking. The mind hive re adapts and traps itself once again and like all bees they will always be at the service of the queen

CYCLOPS SOCIETY

Cyclops, A mythological one eye giant being. Truth requires perspective, without it becomes one sided information. Without a second eye to see the world perspective is lost. A 3D reconstruction of the world is impossible. What happens when you remove perspective from any ideology? What happens when you deny information from any other source to a population? When one religion only is allowed and no other view is permitted? The dark ages. A period which conversion to one sole religion was forced on a population. When any perspective was considered heresy. Blinding society from any other information. What you are being told is the truth and anything else is heresy and punishable by death. But wait didn't McCarthyism in the US worked in similar ways? Didn't Communism in the Soviet Union worked in similar way? This brings us to our question. Is it possible that Communism actually benefited the Prison wall of Capitalism and vice versa? Anyone living in either pole, Capitalism-communism would give their reasons why their side was the best. Country mouse and city mouse discussing about the benefits of their own world WALL. City mouse has been indoctrinated to see the world as CITY MOUSE and will defend the city at all cost against the COUNTRY MOUSE and vice versa. For the WALL to sustain itself a one sided narrative must be fed to its inhabitants. Perspective must be abolished since perspective allows to gain dimension and dimension opens the possibility to see in a more clear perspective. You need two eyes to grasp depth in an image. If you only watch through one eye you limit the information the brain can receive.

By dividing the world in opposing poles the invisible WALL gains once again its big bad wolf and the wall rises to protect its citizens from the horrors of what lays outside its walls.

Of course anyone living inside the wall can't understand what really occurs outside its walls. It has never seen the other side of the wall. It knows only what it has been told. Music, films literature solidify the idea of the big bad wolf living outside the wall. Propaganda machinery selling you reasons why you are better inside your own little world. So society now accepts the bad wolf is going to eat you. You need to work and protect that wall till death because the Wolf is lurking for ways to attack those who live inside the wall. Meanwhile in the opposite side they nourish also their own monster. And that monster even eats its own children and wants to eat your children too. So each of opposing forces builds a bigger wall, they raise flags and fight to protect you from the evil monster. Monsters are fashioned and refashioned keeping its modern slave tucked inside their blankets listening horror stories of what one another will do if their WALL ever came down.

Of course sooner or later the monster needs to change. You can't have people scared of a Kraken forever.

New monsters need to happen and new creatures are born.

Society in turn is forced to accept the reality of the world it is allowed to see with one eye. A blind man's reality is limited to the perception of his senses.

The reality of people in the middle ages was that the world was flat, plagues were divine punishment and witches were to be blamed for illnesses. Monastic religion was the only unquestionable sore towards salvation. Any thought or book that spoke of a different perspective was considered heresy and punishable by death. If you told any of those living in that perceived reality that space travel was possible and that the world wasn't actually flat you would probably get burned for witchcraft. The acceptance of new blocks of construction of reality are limited based on the perception one is allowed to see.

Sides are taken and no other side must be heard. The word Treason is soon used to depict anyone who seeks for perspective or doesn't agree with the one sided information.

Society is then kept under a leash with a simple phrase "Are you with us or against us." No middle ground is allowed. No negotiation or debate.

DISNEYLAND MODEL TO CREATE REALITY

Let's imagine a child was born inside the Disney Park. The child never left that world and the only literature he was allowed to read was fairytales, any other form of literature was banned and considered a form of treason to the ideals that the theme park holds. (Example, Banning Communist literature in the west, banning capitalist literature in the east) The child would grow up to salute the Mickey Mouse flag and to sing the Mickey anthem. He now believes so passionately that Disney is the greatest nation and place that he would fight to death to protect it. Of course once in a while terrible news of the outside Disney world would emerge, solidifying his idea and knowledge that the outside world is filled with horrors. The films he sees portray an evil monstrous foreigner coming to destroy his universe. His entire knowledge of reality is that there is Giant walking stuffed mouse, that the world has parades and fireworks. His knowledge of the world outside is nonexistent or is depicted as grey and filled with sorrow. Disney reality becomes like Blinders in horses. Blinders are placed so the horse can only focus on the road ahead. The road that the rider chose the horse to take.

After all you need that horse to function properly for you. You need that horse to only serve the purpose you designed for him. Limit the horse's perception.

Let him see what you want him to see. Nothing more nothing less. Whip it to keep the horse moving if he slows down. If the man doesn't pay his taxes, have the perfect home, raise a family and work in the perfect job then the horse isn't functioning as it was trained to be. You need the horse to rest or it dies and if the horse dies you lose the slave workforce. Then again the Horse knows no other reality. The horse thanks its master for keeping him safe from the monsters outside the barn. Back to the Disney world. For that world and its population to function properly, all contact with what lays outside its walls must be banned.

But Banning creates instantly rebellious kids. Everyone wants what it cannot have or what is forbidden. So you need to convince the Disney citizen that Nation Disney is the best thing to belong to. You tell him how lucky he is to have been born in Disney. Stockholm syndrome soon kicks in and even if your captor is a cruel sadistic SOB, you simply accept its for your own good. After all, everything they do is for your own good, and everyone around you agrees Disney is the best even if none of them have ever been outside Disney.

Questioning the goodness of being part of Disney now goes unchecked and acceptance of its greatness and the reality that the only way to live is the Disney way. Meanwhile you get tickets for the amusement park every day you can so you forget to question that there might be something outside the Disney WALLS.

Molding society under the fear of a big bad wolf named communism, China, or whatever new monster rises would certainly create a wall of reality in which the demons outside the wall of DISNEY were horrifying and threatened the free world. Anyone born inside such walls of reality knew no other reality nor had a different point of perception except what he was told. What he is being told becomes his reality and thus it becomes canon.

After WW2 world had to rebuild itself. The monster of Fascism and Nazis had ended. A new monster had to be fashioned and molded for the wall to subsist. So the big bad Wolf of communism emerged and after communism new monsters had to be fashioned.

Without opposing poles the wall can't sustain itself. It needs monsters against to fight to protect itself. The threat of Communism or immigrants is indoctrinated and harvested. The nuclear war was coming. The immigrants are coming to take your way of life, be frightened.

Be scared be very scared because they will take your kids and eat them for breakfast. So once again we come to the point in which society has fear imprinted in its core and requires it to keep the bees under a beehive control.

In a certain period of time people thought witches existed and evil curses were the cause of sickness. They weren't considered insane ideas because it was social consensus those things existed. Reality and what is acceptable is carried out by consensus. To deny the existence of witchcraft could put you in the path to be singled out as a witchcraft worshiper.

WELCOME TO THE NUCLEAR ERA SHOW

In 1952 a nuclear bomb explosion was televised from the Nevada desert, In this grand show of horror, dummy homes were built and filled with mannequins of what a common American family looked like. The bomb exploded turning in seconds the house and its smiling mannequin occupants into smithereens. Millions of Americans watching in absolute fear what threat they could face. This could be you! Question now rises. What was the purpose behind such fear induced act? Why frighten a population? The fear of big bad wolf is coming for you. Fear once again allows for policy to be established. The Shadow of communism and the shadow of atomic annihilation. "Be afraid, be very afraid. Now that we got your attention with such terrifying blast, Now that we have mutilated your piece of mind, we now will tell you what is best for you. We can proceed to do what's best for you. Do not worry fellow citizens, we will get rid of the big bad wolf. Its easier to control a population once you remove their continuity of safety. People went off to consider the Soviet Union the greatest threat to their way of living. Even though the US was and has been the only country to ever bomb civilians with nuclear warfare, somehow that wasn't important as long as the threat was seen from outside. The big phantom menace lurking to eat your kids. And so the era of nuclear war was sold on TV for everyone to see, fear and panic. Drills were carried out in schools and workplaces. Monsters that keep the idea that inside the walls you live it is safe. These walls protect you from monsters and demons that will eat babies for breakfast.

Hide the truth with people's own ignorance.

Let us pretend aliens did in fact come to earth. (Pretend for educational purposes only) Do you deny it or you allow the uneducated to send misinformation for you? It's easy to make people reject and not question things when the idea in question is filled with ridiculous associations and statements. Green goblin look alike creatures and people wearing tinfoil helmets to protect you from aliens reading your mind quickly becomes entangled with big foot and soon any sane person questioning and searching for a scientific answer becomes trapped in the conspiracy theory reptilian big foot anti vaccine implanted chip control theory. Its as if Christopher Columbus searching to discover a way to the indies and any conversation he had was engulfed in sirens, Kraken, Sea monsters and the city of Atlantis. The quest for truth soon turns to a series of conversations you could easy find in a mental institution. People due to fear of belonging to the group that wears tinfoil hats will reject any association to ideas that are tainted by ignorance and won't even consider that behind layers of misinformation there could be partial truth. For centuries people claimed the world was flat. Any dissident voices claiming world was not flat were ridiculed and punished for blasphemy. In modern society you allow flat earthers to roam the land with conspiracy theories as fantastic and insane as reptilians because it allows the majority of the population living behind the social wall to reject any questions of what they are being told and therefore the truth is buried behind so many insane theories that it becomes almost impossible to uncover what is real and what isn't. Because conspiracy theories are easy to formulate and always find ways to connect dots in a Schizophrenic manner, without the slightest examination of scientific analysis. Due to research actual data is difficult to find the more ignorant will base their theories by association. Ridiculous examples occur as Red is the color the devil in a painting so if Kanye West dresses Red then he must be a devil worshiper. Ignorance is left to roam freely. I helps create disinformation.

So in the end everything is covered by so much garbage and disinformation that truth could be sitting in plain sight and now one knows if it's true because it has been contaminated by infinite ignorant associations and theories. In the end, do you accept reality as it is being presented to you or do you join the reptilian flat earth mental institution group?

And question rises. What if someone comes out to speak the truth threatening the established order? What if an Anonymous Robin Hood liberator comes out? What then?

The misfortune of hiding behind a mask is the heroic Robin Hood needs to remain ANONYMOUS to protect his identity from the big bad wolf. You need to even ask yourself if the lunching circus act is just a distractor and decoy for the real trick hidden inside the magician's magic hat. Now let's assume the ANONYMOUS Robin Hood is genuinely fighting for his brothers in distress. It's very easy to misdirect his fight by incorporating Robin Hood 2 and Robin Hood 3 and so on until there are so many Robin Hoods out there, some more violent than others, some giving wrong directions to the point that no one actually knows anymore who is who and what is true anymore. People soon become tired, saturated. Cry wolf a thousand times and no one will listen again.

Like any good lawyer you create reasonable doubt to defend the guilty client. Overflowing information with contradictory ideas. A multiple choice test with 100 choices and 1 truth. Some choices sound more credible than the rest and others sound simply insane. Truth becomes hidden under a flow of over information. Conspiracy theories that contradict each other.

Under that scenario, the show becomes boring. What people really want is to go to the beach, party and get laid, not fight an everlasting war especially when everything is clouded by eternal fog and dark corners of misinformation. In the end the majority of beings will end its freedom fighting quest and return to its cage to sleep once again. The freedom fighting fashion becomes a T-shirt, the book everyone carries to impress the girl next door hoping it will help him to get laid and maybe post a few hashtags and selfies to pretend they care just for the sake of attaching themselves to an idea that they are different, good, and smarter than the rest. They can now identify themselves to a branded idea and buy all the proper equipment and gadgets that go with that life style they convince themselves it represents who they are.

EVERYTHING YOU SAY CAN BE AND WILL BE USED AGAINST YOU IN THE SOCIAL COURT

Freedom of speech is one of those things that is good as an idea but really never carried out in practice.

Society and its need to protect its fashionable morality and set of indoctrinated beliefs removes instantly any freedom of speech. Freedom of speech with a contract in small letters that states "As long as it doesn't contradict or offend the established social order".

Beauty of how that contract works in the invisible prison is no law will imprison those who dare speak their minds and contradict the established order. Society will simply shame those with different opinions into submission. Few decades ago if anyone showed support and spoke in favor of the Gay community, most likely they would be silenced and shamed into submission for speaking up their minds. They had their right to freedom of speech but in practice social censorship would punish them for doing so. Decades ago any support for interracial marriage or black community could mean you could kiss your career goodbye. Freedom of speech is an illusion to keep people inside the WALL under a false idea that they are free. Anything that is said that contradicts or endangers the SOCIAL ESTABLISHMENT will not be punished by law but by being outcast from the social group and its benefits. Instantly being sent to social Siberia for speaking unpopular ideas. In the Communist era especially North Korean dictatorship it was seen by those who committed the crime of contradicting the dictator or questioning its rules or practices.

 The felon who spoke freely was sentenced and its family thrown into shame and misery. In western society government doesn't impose such measures. It's Society the Judge and Juror. Dare to speak against the establishment and memes and public shaming will be used against you. Actors that have been fired for shows due to their ideas. Mel Gibson Shamed and ridiculed constantly by Ricky Gervais while everyone points its finger in support of Gervais for doing so. List goes on and on. How the social prison is well guarded by its citizens all in the service of its fashionable morality and sense of self-righteousness.

People in their need to protect the illusory PRISON WALLS they live in will fight to death to sustain the idea to which they attached themselves to. The induced idea at first is foreign and the subject is then tricked to think it agrees with the idea so the idea is now his. It is how people are made to believe in GOD, COUNTRY, BRANDS and PEOPLE.

Flags, fashion, brands and celebrities rise as a symbol of the self and that which defines the individual and once the self is attached to ideas it will use self-preservation mechanisms to defend the idea that was implanted on him. If the beloved idol or brand disappoints its follower it will unleash the inner self-preservation mechanism to protect the self and its emotional investment in the idol. Since no being can go against itself due to natural self-preservation instincts, the object once loved becomes repelled with fury in order to detach it from the self. The idol needs now to be destroyed to warranty self-preservation. If the act of ultimate destruction isn't carried out, moral or physical suicide is required to preserve intact the being and avoid further suffering.

THE PIT OF HOPE
Bread and Circus

Humanity thrives on a sense of identity and purpose within the world at large. Humans require experiences such as tension, stress, anxiety and the need to survive to engage in society. Without them the social construct deteriorates and when all needs are accounted for, and no conflict exists, the act of living is stripped to its primal physiological essence of food and sleep. Therefore you push society to fight for daily subsistence. Like any other beast of labor must work shifts to pay its right to live. Labor society trades minutes and hours of their perishing limited life for trading chips in the game of life.

As most people in this word, they must go through a series of tasks along a tiresome repetitive routine called work. Most just waiting for Friday to arrive so they can exchange their chips traded for hours of their lives for some kind of entertainment and a dose of numbing alcohol and the occasional smoke of CTB.

 Some beasts of labor head back to their own modern cave shelters of brick and mortar. Ready themselves for cover from the darkness of night. Some get ready for their daily dose of televised morphine. As all machines of labor, these machines must rest, feed and participate in recreational and procreation endeavors.

We don't want the machine to break down so we give you todays marvel. 160,000 channels of same shit just in different packages. Don't worry your opinion means a lot to us. You are important! Statistic of preprogramed response to the entertainment morphine.

Some engage in ritualistic observance of a numbing box called T.V. others prefer smaller numbing boxes called mobile phones with social apps that flash the lives of other beasts of labor and we call it SOCIAL NETWORKS, others engage in game simulations that induce its players into a comatose state of simulated victory and glory.

In the end what all these have in common is they release the tension with a simulation of free will. You chose how you spend your time off after work. If these forms of simulations did not occur the social machine would break down. The paid enslaved workforce would rebel at any or all rules given to them. Their need for escape would spread like fire. Protests on massive scale would occur for the simplest reasons. Countries with less opportunities in life have longer holidays, Marginalized societies have far more recreational activities which makes them less inclined to protest their miserable working conditions and insufficient salary.

The Roman poet Juvenal stated Bread and circus as a way Romans controlled the masses. Without the modern circus, the workforce would rebel not because of its working conditions but because of lack of windows in its cell. That window comes in the form of games, sports, concerts, alcohol, sex and any recreational activity. Remove circus and the social establishment will fall. Circus numbs and keeps the crowd constantly fed with its dose of dopamine, it releases the tension on caged animals. There's nothing wrong in attending a circus event. It's quite healthy to do so. What is unhealthy is to not see its use in social domestication. If you don't put a small valve in the pressure pot the pressure pot will explode.

In solitary confinement the prisoner placed on an enclosed window quickly loses its sense of reality taking the prisoner down a spiral that deteriorates his mind, becoming increasingly violent anxious and sooner or later the situation loses control with authority and other inmates. If the prisoner is given the chance to go out and has activities that distract his imprisonment the prisoner becomes far more docile and is easier to control. Windows of hope are given to inmates. Hope becoming a simulation of freedom.

Society works in similar ways. To keep its citizens docile it needs to provide windows of hope and windows of distraction. Windows that allow the social inmates inside the WALLS of society to scream, shout and release the tension of their invisible incarceration.

Remove the escape of entertainment and sports events and soon you will have protests, rebellion and lynching for any cause that pops up. Freedom fighters will rise for any cause and motive and the fire will spread. They would claim it's for a just cause which certainly it would be, but most likely they would be less inclined to revolt if the escape valve had not been closed.

CREATING THE MIRAGE OF HOPE

Hope. A word that implies a promise of light at the end of the tunnel. Without hope or even a glimpse of it, the human will cracks down. Chaos emerges. In a world without hope, preservation of moral and order is no longer required. If there's no hope of leaving the dumpster then there's no reason to strive anymore nor to comply with moral. You end in a Mad Max ruthless society where its inhabitants eat one another to satisfy their instantaneous primal needs. Chaos and lawlessness rises. The human instinct becomes primitive and only functions in the pursuit of self-gratification. Therefore Hope must be modeled and fashioned to direct the flock towards the light and desires one wishes them to see. And so what hope do you induce? Humanity in general never knows what it wants, it needs a menu to be crafted out for them. Without the guidance into a preprogramed hope an ideal will sooner or later rise among the population, an Ideal that could crumble the established order. Emerald city even as a lie must prevail to keep the quest. Long term hopes extinguishes rapidly due to lack of discipline so the flock conforms to whatever crumbs it can obtain. So in this simulation of hope, reflectors turn to talent shows and success stories that fill TV programs and magazines.

AMERICA'S GOT TALENT
THE SIMULATION OF HOPE

TV Screens flash the recent want to be Pop star, performing in expected ridicule for the Circus entertainer Simon and his talent show. The modern gladiatorial spectacle for the bored masses has begun. A contest meant to shame the least talented who's only mistake was to read too many inspirational quotes and have daddy tell them they were meant for greatness. As any gladiatorial match, there is a Cesar, now a modern day buffoon entertainer named Simon and his gang of jurors also known as unemployed once used to be pop star singers. The crowd listens to the poor bastard who dared think he could sing outside his shower. And so after a disastrous performance the Cesar Simon and ex pop stars will give a verdict "thumbs up thumbs down" on the poor modern day gladiator AKA Wannabe performer. Audience awaits the nasty verdict with a blood thirst delight. A modern thumbs down turned into the sentence. THAT WAS ABSOLUTELY TERRIBLE! Crowd pleased or shocked by the ruthless comments the Cesar Simon inflicts on his gladiators.

Of course the gladiatorial spectacle would not work at all if all Gladiators fail the trials. So you look for the most underdog figure you can find. The bullied skinny kid with large glasses or the low self-esteem girl whose sole appearance cracks jokes as she timidly walks into the arena. And then it's when the magic occurs. The low self-esteem bullied gladiator marvels the bully audience. Cameras focus on the surprise of the Jurors (You need to show how surprised everyone is because of the bullied underdog for the trick to work) The audience gets its dose of dopamine and self-compassion mirrored through the underdog who defied all expectations to succeed in the Arena of entertainment. It gives the illusion to the underdog entertained crowd that they can also escape their dire situation into stardom like the gladiator. Fame and fortune they could obtain if only they eat their peas and vegetables, work hard and pay their taxes on time. . The audience can now believe that they too have hope. Those prisoners locked in a pit soon gain hope once again.

A pit requires a shaft of light for its prisoners to not lose their minds. An illusion of hope. Underdog girl who they themselves bullied towards failure suddenly becomes a beacon of light in their prison.

An inspirational commercial to sell you the Idea "You can do it" even though the game was created to minimize all chances of you succeeding. Underdog stories keep the modern slaves under a leash so they can trade their lives for chips with the illusion that there is an escape. If the mirage of an escape isn't given the modern slaves lose hope and chaos rises. Its hope that keeps rebellions at bay. Slaves work better when given a window that gives them hope after their long hours of tolerating the sadistic boss. Slavery works better when slavery is hidden from plain sight. You trade the whip for bills to pay. You trade daily rations and call them minimum wage and make them work harder to get better daily rations but still they are just daily rations traded by giving up their quickly perishing life. Give the modern slave just enough to keep the mouse running on its wheel indefinitely until the mouse is of no use to the system and is retired. And so underdog stories give purpose and legend of the skinny mouse who escaped its prison emerges. Inspirational quotes flood the web and underdog is paraded through cat walks and shows as living proof there is escape as long as you follow the rules given to you. The simulation is now real.

 A simulation that numbs the social core that freedom and equal chances actually exists. A simulation carried out in every red carpet event and Premier convincing wannabe actors and show biz dreamers that they too can stand in a red carpet under glimmering lights with smiles glued to one's face saying "Hey look at me." Of course the reflectors don't show the other half a million souls that had to quit their dreams because chances of entrance to the elite group is closed. Without the spectacle, the magic trick can't work.

Without Banksy pulling a regular stunt like shredding a painting, his work would get lost among the millions of artworks of better artistic value posted on a daily basis on Instagram that get little to no attention. Showbiz to simulate that there is a way out.

— **The Black Coffee Axiom** —

IMPLANTING IDEAS

Ideas can be implanted into society, these implants mold the fabric of how the modern lab rat behaves and consumes.

The phrase "Science Says" removes doubt from the child community. It's like saying grownups know better than you. It forces people to accept any statement without even being put into question. Who are the scientists in question? What study was conducted and under which conditions were they studied becomes instantly irrelevant.

Scientific method requires observation of a phenomenon, Question and formulate a   Hypothesis resulting in Experimentation (Trial and error) to give a conclusion. Of course the term Science says nullifies in the social flock the individual scientific method of finding the truth. It makes people assume and take as absolute what is being told to them without need of individual verification.

We arrive to what could seem as an innocent headline. "Science says people who drink black coffee might be psychopaths. You don't want to be a psychopath, so better add more sugar and some milk just to be sure". From now on be worry of anyone who drinks its coffee black. The idea has been planted. A simple idea that removes personal preference and soon becomes an idea to keep track of other people's behavior. No need to verify the information since it specifically says SCIENCE SAYS. Of course people don't have time to go through data and meticulous investigation to find out if the headline is in fact true. Headline says "Science says" so why bother investigate, scientists already did it for you.

Its validity and science behind such statement becomes accepted because of an ANONYMOUS source called Science says. A nobility title meant to trick people to not question what is said to them. After all the general romanticized idea is Scientists carry hundreds of books you will never read or understand, they have glasses and robes and have a higher knowledge of things than the rest. Therefore don't question Authority. They know better than you. Accept what is being told to you without doubt. Once most of the population as been inoculated with an Idea, the Idea becomes canon and therefore reality. Truth is no longer necessary since the general belief is what matters.

From there on anyone caught drinking black coffee will be instantly branded as a possible Psychopath. The idea will surface in the subconscious each time a black coffee drinker is seen, Such thought will alter irremediably the individual conduct to avoid being flagged as a psychopath or whatever the inoculated thought that was given be it Black coffee, dressing in black, reading certain literature or more profound ideas and behavior.

Such implant of Ideas and behavior patterns can be seen in government institutions, Celebrities speaking for causes, O.M.S., Bill Gates or the Tom Hanks likable actor to promote an Idea. When you least know it you have the new Tom Hanks commercial.

One of those very annoying commercials but with a
sticky tune. Tom Hanks Appears on Screen,
America's favorite actor. Nothing can go wrong with
Tom Hanks. He smiles with Oscar winning elegance
and sells to the flock whatever new behavior pattern
they need to learn and since its Tom Hanks then it
must be true. Everyone wants to have a Tom Hanks
father figure to listen and tell them what's better for
them. Role models working in service of the prison
wall.

THE PUPPET SHOW

"How clear everything becomes when you look from
the darkness of a dungeon."

-Umberto Eco, Foucault's Pendulum-

Humanity is very similar to any puppet, Pull a string
and a limb moves, Pull another string and a different
limb moves and soon you have the puppet walking
and dancing at the speed and tune the puppet master
wishes it to move. Like any animal it can be trained.
The trick for how to train society is to convince the
puppet that it was his idea to move and dance at the
tune it was given.

To break free requires consciousness and constant questioning of why to comply with the established order. Questions like. Why do people do what they do and why is a tune being played?

Why is something being indoctrinated? Is something just a fashionable moral or does it really represent everlasting good? Why is everyone dancing to the same tune? Without WHY you turn into a reactive zombie. You remain numb as sheep headed towards the slaughter house. Wasting time not knowing that time was the only thing anyone could afford to lose.

Reaction is the basis of social media. Want people to become involved with something that was posted? Then make them react emotionally. Publish a video of cat being slaughtered with a click bait headline "Neighbor caught on camera killing cat" You have captured emotionally the attention of the crowd and now they simply react. Emotions take over not allowing any intelligent judgment. Simple reactive puppets will burst into pure emotion.

To see things as they really are you need to take distance, Emotions remove distance and make people take them personal therefore they become reactors.

Taking distance allows you to see how things really are. You can't know how the earth really looks if you are standing on it, you can't know if its round or flat. You have to go to outer space to see its shape and how it really looks. Take distance from it. You can only see what a mountain looks like if you can see the mountain from a distance. As long as you become involved emotionally with what is told and presented to you, you can't know the truth and you will move and dance at the tune you are given.

Society moves at the tune that it is given. Fear will in the end lead individuals to give up their individuality in order to belong to the flock. It is seen when students bully into submission those who seem different or have different ideas, The consensus mind hive forces into submission everyone under its own view of the world of fashionable morality and values it has accepted as valid. In such model it is decided what races or sexual preferences or religion and spiritual beliefs are acceptable or not. What can be said and what cannot. The submission model is indoctrinated by fashionable group thinking. The collective mind is there to enforce justice and punishment to all those who step out of line. The social justice fighters go from victims to victimizer. From liberators to oppressors. Anyone with different opinion soon becomes target of those who first saw themselves as seekers of justice and freedom. All this in a necessity of adapting and making the social puppets comply willingly or by force to the social model of the time.

In the end everyone will have to dance at the tune they are given if they wish to remain inside the safety and establishment. Comply or be outcast outside the invisible wall of society.

9 798655 237759